The Zero Years

The Zero Years

A Book of Poems

Domenic Blair

ISBN-13: 9780692469439
ISBN-10: 0692469435

Table Of Contents

Her Smile

Just seeing your smile
The first time we ever met
Made me fall for you

Always Missing You

It must have been your smile
That made me start to wonder
How far I would drive
Just to see you love the summer

As soon as I saw your eyes
I felt my heart start singing
Suddenly I felt alive
But I probably stopped my breathing

And the magic of your hips
Made every part of me start wishing
That I could learn to dance
So we could share a musical evening

Something about those lips
Made my mind and heart start thinking
That if I could get close enough
I could hear you whisper me your secrets

Maybe it's just a crush
Since I barely know your name
But what if this is love
Could you ever feel the same

What if I'm not good enough
For you to notice me
Should I be giving up
Or are we meant to be

In case it doesn't show
I'm not sure on what to do
All I really know
Is that I'm always missing you

Marvelously Silent

I am still here
Next to you
Trying to find a word to say
My tongue seems lost
And I don't know what to do

You are still here
Next to me
But also racing through my mind
Your smile looks marvelous
I probably don't deserve it

We are still here
Next to each other
Not saying a word
And it's the greatest feeling
Saying absolutely nothing

Yellow Neon Lights

The party is loud
But only you exist
Somehow I hear you
Every word
And every laugh

As close as I can get
Almost enough to touch your skin
While you talk to me
And we exist somewhere else

The street is noisy
But somehow perfectly quiet
At least when you speak
It's a perfect night
Because you are here with me

You are wearing my jacket
Because you shivered a little
And it's the closest thing
That I can get
To me wrapping my arms around you

We enter a building
With yellow neon lights
To watch a band play
I don't remember the music
I just remember you

Before we go our separate ways
You tell me to call you
With your number now on my hand
And your arms around my neck
I can only smile at the thought of seeing you again

Her Taste

The love that we give
With our bodies and our souls
Is very precious

New Addiction

The rush I get from holding your hand
And being able to look into your eyes
A feeling only you and I understand

Just being so physically close
Causes many thoughts to race through my mind
And more when we are alone

I can't explain the sensation
Of finally kissing you
I feel something beyond elation

There's such a heavy tension
From what our bodies want to do
Something both of us won't mention

We are close enough to share a breath
And our heart beats start to sync
I want all of you and nothing less

The rest of the world doesn't matter
As long as your lips are this close to me
I just want to hear your whispers and laughter

The Zero Years

Our kisses become more alive
We hold each other a little tighter
I feel my animalistic urges start to rise

Attraction gaining strength
And inhibitions becoming lighter
With every new breath we give and take

Energy Thieves

I dare myself to grab your hand
Our fingers now interlaced
Skin on skin
Sharing energy

While I mentally celebrate this moment
Your lips are suddenly on mine
Those lips I have dreamed about
That tongue I'm suddenly enjoying

A little more and you start to moan
Your teeth biting my lip
Stealing each others breath
Tasting each other's energy

I pull you on top of me
And we use our hands to find more
More skin, more warmth
More everything

Using my mouth to explore more of you
I follow the path my hands have taken
Gaining wisdom of each other
Discarding clothes and shame

You are now my favorite taste in the world
With your moans as my favorite song
Between your thighs I become alive
We become a shared source of energy

Your lips find mine again
Stealing your flavors back from me
You get back on top and don't hesitate
As I feel myself slowly going into you

A little faster as more of us combine
With our teeth leaving marks on each other
Trying to take as much as we can
Stealing each other's energy

The Sleeping Perfection

As you fall asleep in my arms
Your soft skin bare for me to caress
I can only admire your natural beauty as art
You are a living masterpiece and nothing less

Watching the glow of the TV screen
Dance across your body of perfection
Like an ocean of colors continuously moving
On a canvas made from heaven

Every inch of you that I observe
Is another detail I find amazing
The electric glow follows your curves
Jealous of what I'm embracing

I whisper how you have my heart
And kiss your lips as gently as the lights
I feel at peace with where we are
As you smile and squeeze me tight

Affectionate Goddess

The look you give
Right before we kiss
A permanent image on my mind

Your passionate moans
As we connect bodies and souls
Is the most beautiful song in life

Just the way we are
Listening to each other's hearts
Is how I want to spend forever

How you whisper to me
As we fall asleep
Makes my dreams so much better

Disappearing Act

Please don't disappear
There are so many moments
That we need to share

Thorns

You are a rose
And I love you the way you are

I will not take you away
And strip you of your thorns
Or put you in a vase
And pretend it's your home

You won't be on display
Like something I can own
I love you in every way
I will try to help you grow

You are a rose
And I love you the way you are

Please don't disappear
Just because the winter is cold
I will help you, have no fear
I don't want to be all alone

What we had is already gone
You are not here anymore
I would have gladly held you in my arms
Just to keep you safe and warm

You were a rose
And I loved you the way you were

Alternate Echo

In a different universe
We would be together
In another timeline
Things would be so perfect
Little changes here
Alternate words said there
In some other life
I would still be with you

Instead of just an echo
Falling to the silence
Instead I'm a ghost
Fading into space
Everyday repeats
With you forgetting me
In your world
I no longer exist

Tasteless Cupcake

My senses are starting to fail me
How else do I explain it
The sudden lack of life all around
Surely I am starting to decay
One sensation at a time

Moving on
As every vibrant color
Starts fading to gray
The bursts of the sun's radiance is gone
Lights and shadows become more similar

The world around me loses all distinction
Every sound becomes the same
No more difference between laughing and crying
My ears can't detect the nuances in music
Somehow everything is monotone

From flowers and rain
To dirt and decay
No aroma stands out
Nothing worth following
Worth trying to find as a scented candle

Everything is cold
No matter what day of summer it is
Or what the thermometers read
Soft blankets and pillows
Are so similar to gravel and pavement

My tongue no longer works
From the frosting on cupcakes
To the most bitter pill
It is all the taste of paper
And just as nourishing

Maybe my senses are failing
Because she disappeared on me
And she is all I ever desired
Everything else is lifeless
Since she took my happiness with her

She made my world come alive
With that beautiful smile and joyful laugh
And her sweet fragrance
Only matched by the taste of her soft lips
She was my everything

I will stay this way forever
Listening to old songs with deafening ears
Watching it all turn to the same tasteless gray
Trying to remember how to enjoy a cupcake
Hoping that this one is just stale

Back To The Madness Of Reality

The world I live in
Is just a constant nightmare
And you were a dream

Gone

She's not sitting in the past
Patiently waiting
I don't know why I keep searching there

She's not wearing something beautiful
And a smile just for me
Maybe I should stop dreaming of her

I'm just digging into memories
Past the scars and the pain
Missing the love that I still need

I don't know if there's any hope
To love her again or move on
But I'm stuck here thinking for now

Reckless

I get into my car
My proof of success
Hard work and dedication
I don't deserve less

My favorite color
The best thing in my life
Speakers as loud as the engine
Time for a drive

I hate how it's empty
There's never a passenger
No one is ever waiting
When the trips are over

I can speed up forever
No voice will tell me to stop
The perfect contraption
And I hate every moving part

My crowning achievement
Is just so damn hollow
Such a shiny coffin
For the road I follow

Days into nights
And alone I will age
Surrounded by things
Stuff I can replace

I decide to accelerate
This machine that can't feel
Aim it at my shallow legacy
And let go of the wheel

I'm waiting to crash
Into the walls I made exist
My eyes will stay open
I don't plan to flinch

Infinite Negative Loop

I am weak because I am worthless
I am worthless because I am nothing
I am nothing because I am weak

The constant noise only I hear
Always seems to get louder
The silent feedback is deafening
Consuming every thought I have

Taking away my balance
Crushing what I am internally
I can't hear my world around me
My whole body begins to fail

The air in my lungs becomes scarce
My vision borders on turning black
I was right, I am weak
I am worthless, I am nothing

Mechanical

I don't feel pain anymore
I just watch what destroys me
Movement lacking thought
Output the only purpose
Hollow and efficient

I've become something mechanical
A device that barely has needs
Functions not meant for love
Working till I'm lifeless
And death the final position

Running On Empty

Everything hurts
And nothing matters
I faced today
Before I finished yesterday
It all blurs together
But the dark spots remain clear

I'm running on empty
With no place to stop
Mostly falling forwards
Somehow not crashing
Nothing tries to catch me
And I can't catch my breath

I'm just always staring
At my life in the mirror
The endless road I'm on
Or the blank ceiling above my bed
Never at a dream
Or something that makes me happy

I'm still pushing on
But I'm falling apart at the seams
It would be so obvious
To stop and breathe
If I knew how I wouldn't be here
Waiting to collide with anything

Automated Noose

My life stuck inside a circle
That gets tighter and tighter
Around my neck

It gets harder to breathe
As days go faster
In front of me

I can't pull my head out
I'm losing my air
Till there's nothing left

I can't feel my support
The ground gets farther
From my feet

Lost And Found

I do not know why
You left and came back to me
But I missed your smile

Sad Again

Here we are
Living a life apart
One of us is happy
The other is always in misery

You only call me on a sad day
And I show up to take the clouds away
You never want to share your sunshine
At least not with my life

I give you all the good that I can
And take every ounce of your sad
I guess I am just a secret
The keeper of your regrets

I love you so I never move on
You take my heart when you are gone
So I'm here barely trying to live
Until you are sad again

Fake The Smile

I see you again
Not in a dream
Yet somehow you are not here
At least your smile isn't
Because I dreamed of you
A thousand times

This isn't you
Wearing a paper mask
The perfectly drawn smile
Almost as beautiful as the real thing
And your eyes are so lifeless
But the right color

I know it's fake
I can see the tear stains
Bleeding through
Ruining what you created
Yet somehow only I noticed
Despite everyone who looks your way

You fake the smile
But you run to me
And I don't know why
You are here
Why did you disappear
And why are you back

I wish I could scream at you
For leaving me
And showing up
As soon as the dreams stopped
Like you knew
I started to move on

But your paper mask
Starts to fall away
You have been hurt
And I feel so confused
Do I let you cry
Or try to find your real smile

Quiet

Tell me yes
Tell me no
Tell me anything

The sweetest lie
The most painful truth
This quiet is suffocating

Say you're sorry
Say you're not
Just say something soon

Swear at me
Laugh in my face
I just want to hear from you

Storms

After the storms
Have left my heart
Thinking of you
Makes it restart

Knowing your smile
Gives beauty to the day
Is like knowing the sun
Will follow the rain

We lost each other
In a terrible flood
I hope I find you
And we can share our love

It will take time
But the storms will pass
We can survive this
And the love will last

Golden Moments

We can be happy
With love, trust, and commitment
As a family

As Fireworks Burst

The sun gives way to darkness
But we stay outside
The sound of artificial thunder
Brings our attention to the sky

We look up in wonder
As fireworks burst
We ignore our tragic tomorrows
And forget about yesterday's hurt

I watch for your smile
In the flashes of light
Our grief is gone for a while
On this magical night

Sparks of different colors
Erase our damaging thoughts
The celebration brings us together
When it all seemed lost

Loud booms and laughter
Echo into the street
The silence is coming
But now you are next to me

As the final sparks diminish
Our smiles still remain
This night may be finished
But we still have more to celebrate

Little Star

My little star
I'm doing my best to keep you glowing
Even if the shadows keep on growing
In the sea of stars I will always pick you

My little star
You won't face the dark alone
I will watch you and give you a home
I will be here till you are brighter than the sun

My little star
You are a spark that will guide me
To a world that will make you happy
I will build a telescope just to watch you

With My Hands

I will show you love
You show me trust
I will learn everything about you

From how you play
To what keeps you safe
There is so much that we can do

Against the world
That can be so cruel
I will guard you from the unlovable

As the years start to fly
And you grow by my side
Nothing will ever be impossible

I must do what I can
To provide with my hands
I will do my best every single day

You are just a child
But just for a while
And I promise to never go away

I will always keep up
As you learn to run
And I will cheer as you succeed

And if you ever fall
I will give it my all
To show how much you still mean to me

Foundation

I couldn't be happier
Than I am now
Being with you and your kids
Laughing out loud

Those two will never look like me
And I don't even care
They are perfect the way they are
They don't need my messy hair

Learning what food they like
And how to help you when you get overwhelmed
Are just some of the things I promise to do
I am dedicated to our happiness and health

Whatever I have ever possessed
In my life before we were together
Is worth giving up and selling
So their happiness will last forever

The tireless effort of being a family
Has been my greatest joy
I love waking up next to you
On a couch surrounded by toys

I may not have been in those pictures
Taken so long ago
But I would love to build us a foundation
And we can all share a life and a home

Candy Necklace

I miss the way things used to be
When a small scratch
Was the worst thing to happen to me

When I didn't know what heartbreak was
When all I had and knew
Was just pure happiness and love

Playing in the dirt, kicking a ball
Holding hands and going in circles
Until we would get so dizzy that we would fall

A candy necklace to go with your ring
Pinkie swears and cootie shots
Taking turns in the swings

Legacy

Whatever toys I still have
Are now yours to take
And I will be glad
To sit and watch you play

The stuffed rabbit I would hold
To keep me feeling safe
During the nights and storms
When I was your age

All the tools that I earned
And what skills I can teach
Can be yours if you want to learn
So you can be better than me

The musical instruments I loved to collect
Are waiting for you to play
They will be kept from neglect
And ready for the stage

What life lessons I have learned
I will pass on to you
You don't need the cuts or burns
The pain I went through

This legacy is yours to own
Whatever it's worth
Build it into a home
I won't leave you with dirt

But if you don't want any of this
That's okay with me
Because your love and happiness
Is the greatest part of my legacy

Travelers

Let's plan our trip
To some place new
You, me and the little passengers
We will follow the road
To a fun and exciting city
Having fun walking new streets
And adding to our stories

Let's go camping
Out in the wild
Just us and the adventurers
Off the beaten path
Until we find a perfect spot
To gather around a fire
Counting stars and laughs

Let's go for a drive
To a sunny beach
Us and the tiny swimmers
Parked near the sand
We can run to the water
Try to ride waves
And build giant sandcastles

Let's keep going
To places we have never been
As a family
With whatever guides us
Let's build moments together
So we can all have fun
Going down memory lane

Let's be travelers

The Last Promise To Break

You should have told me
That it would all end badly
For me and my heart

Ignorance In Devotion

Tell me the words you want me to hear
I will only believe your voice
Despite what other people warn me
I am devoted to you

Feed me enough to use me
I will gladly starve waiting for you
You are all the nourishment I want
I am devoted to you

Your constant poisonings are tasteless
You don't enjoy my suffering anymore
What else can I give for your enjoyment
I am devoted to you

Psychopathic Compassion

If you knew what it felt like
Why did you do it to me
Destroying what we had with a knife
Instead of letting me down gently
You have been here before
The victim of someone's cruelty
But you cut me a little more
While saying you are sorry

You keep giving the knife a twist
But you keep saying it's not your fault
If you knew how to quit
Then why do it at all
You promised to never do the same
Because you knew what it's like to fall
And having to deal with so much pain
So I believed you all along

You just lied without remorse
And played the victim so well
I doubt you can say the truth anymore
Because you keep building this hell
I'm just another victim you don't claim
Another bastard with a lie to sell
Eventually I will go away
Like a true story you forget to tell

Beautiful Liar

You are so perfect for me
If only I could believe you
My beautiful
Liar

I wish you really didn't cheat
That I could deny the truth
My corrupted
Angel

To forgive you would be nice
But this will definitely happen again
My wonderful
Stranger

I wish I didn't waste my time
With trying to love you till the end
My greedy
Lover

Losing

Everyone that I see
Is a rival
That you will always choose
Over me

All that I do
Will never be
Good enough to be noticed
By you

Every flaw I have
Is magnified
Over a thousand times
Are you glad

You will just wait
Till there's more
For you to choose from
Anyways

The castles I construct
Are never enough
For you to want to stay
In love

Burial

You finally hit the bottom
Lost everything to lose
Instead of climbing up
And reaching for an escape
You reach for a shovel
To dig some more

Something about pride
Keeps you down there
Like it's all intentional
A place you want to be
And something you want more of
Because you keep digging

Burying yourself deeper
Making an escape less likely
For no other reason
Killing our hope for you
Having us attend a funeral
And not a celebration

Separating Scars

We were fused together
Because we bled at the same time
Both of us healing and coping
Supporting each other

You broke me off and kept me wounded
Always hurting, always bleeding
So when you need me
I would be too weak to leave

I am just your constant donor
Nothing but your second heart
Your antidote to your vices
The one who suffers for you

The scars are no longer mine
They are yours but I have them
And they just multiply
A little more grotesque every time

Villainous Heroes

All we have
Are these villainous heroes
To save us
For ourselves

We don't want to listen
But we will always beg them
When we are in danger
And we never learn

All we do
Is abuse our saviors
And blame them
For our stupidity

We just ignore them
When they suffer
Their own battles
We just don't care

All I am
Is your villainous hero
That you beg for
And cast away

I just try to catch you
And keep you safe
But you jump back
And jump some more

All I do
Is cure your sickness
And stand there
To take your wrath

You won't ever pay attention
Or return the favor
But I see you
Walk off another edge

Fangs

I don't know how you can just go
From one to another
You are heartless and cold
So I don't think they are lovers

You are some sort of spider
Always spinning a web
A compulsive liar
Someone new in your bed

Some greedy creature
With venomous fangs
Using a woman's beauty and features
Causing anger and pain

You pretended kindness
To get me close enough
Depending on my love's blindness
Until your fangs have used me up

Somehow I survived
But I am far from okay
Because I live my life
With your venom still in my veins

I should have left you broken
When you came back crying to me
Claiming that someone has ripped you open
You were only trying to feed

Fractures: Shattered

Life is a cruel joke
We chase our heart's dreams
With our brittle bones

Frailty

We are composed
Of just flesh and bone
Neither one
Will last too long

Just enough force
And your body contorts
In a way
That goes beyond pain

Ask me how
A shattered bone sounds
Or how the flesh
Looks bruised and dead

Somehow we live naïve
Like our bodies will never bleed
That we are invincible
And we have control

Recovery In Stagnation

The pain should be unbearable
According to everyone
My arm looked so gruesome
The way it was shattered and backwards

The worst part of it should be over
Said the surgeon
The bone now stronger than before
With a plate and screws holding it in place

You should take it easy
Is what I'm being told
By the people whose lives still move
While I'm recovering by myself

The break wasn't that bad
Maybe from the adrenaline
Or just my tolerance
Or compared to my current stagnation

The worst part isn't over
I'm still stuck where I am
Still not able to do anything
Still healing by myself

This is far from easy
Watching the world spin along
I'm just collecting dust
And living in aging memories

Atrophic

Watching myself deteriorate
My hard work becoming a myth
I am still a hostage to the trauma

The ever present scar
Reminding me why I'm here
Why I have to stop and recover

My strength replaced with dead weight
The power I had is gone
I can't wake up from the living nightmare

Fixing The Hidden Broken

Pain
Suffering
Hurt
Weakness

Everybody will experience a broken feeling
No matter how safe and boring a life can be
Or how much armor we wrap ourselves in

Tougher still can be what happens afterwards
During the healing and recovery process
After the trauma is over

We can swap out bandages
Witness scar progression
Count more reps in physical therapy

If only everything that breaks in us was so visual
Easier to measure and given a timeline
Predict when it all should get better

Not everything can be bolted back into place
Stitched together like a stuffed animal
Or strengthened by adding more resistance

Not every trauma leaves an obvious reminder
At least not to strangers
And sometimes not even loved ones

Fractures: Mending

We both seem broken
I will gladly fix your pain
If you will fix mine

To Love And Recover

You have a past to blame
I have a pill to take
Both of us have excuses
Not to love each other

My self-destruction
And your love of corruption
Sound like good reasons
To keep our hands together

Don't add to my scars
I won't break your heart
We can learn to smile
Without needing to suffer

One day at a time
Until we have better lives
And all we will do
Is love and support one another

Soft Crush

Watching your lips move
Pretending I don't miss them
That smile I still dream about

Your voice is still my favorite sound
From your laugh to your moans
To the hypnotic way you say my name

Your skin looking soft to my hands
Sweet to my tongue
And vulnerable to my teeth

I know too much about your body
How your curves look without clothes
What your love and saliva tastes like

Too many memories for me to ignore
Too many images of you on top of me
Too many things we still need to do

You bring me closer and we embrace
The soft crush of your body into mine
I feel our hearts sync like they used to

We could be doing so much more
Touching souls instead of just skin
Sharing sweat instead of just smiles

Deliberate Collapse

I relapse into you
My goddess
My devilish temptation

You dig into my old scars
The happiness
The failed salvation

Same doses as before
Without tolerance
Without any caution

The last bridge has been burned
Lost acceptance
Lost all redemption

Nothing will be gained
Just solace
Just more damnation

I take all that I can consume
Your malice
Your killing elation

Intravenously

I take you
Straight into my veins
Now you are in my heart
And every thought on my brain

I consume you
Deep into my lungs
I taste you on my breath
And I still can't get enough

I fiend for you
My entire body aches
When you disappear
And leave me the pain

I'm lost without you
There's no more life
The world seems empty
No future in my sight

I move on without you
But you are still in my veins and skin
In my heart, brain and lungs
Even if I don't see you again

Damned Salvation

She make-believes
I'm her demon
And her savior
Depends on what she needs

I start to see
The growing horns
Ant the halo
But they are not on me

We try to breathe
But I'm drowning
In her sorrow
I will try not to leave

She wants to grieve
Her broken love
And her horror
I just feel so naïve

She wants to be
Simply happy
And not haunted
I will try to give reprieve

I can't perceive
Her dark torment
Or her salvation
I just wish she was free

Fractures: Necrosis

Something worse than death
Is living when part of you
Has died long ago

Without You

I'm not afraid to live my life without you
To jump out of planes, chase the sun
To drive fast, and climb mountains

I'm not afraid to risk myself
To break bones, and gain scars
To catch fire, to almost drown

I'm afraid of when it's all over
When I look back, when I dream
That it's you I think about, you I remember

I'm afraid that it will be you I miss
When I get old, when the end draws near
Despite a lifetime, and years without you

Rx

What pill do I need
To make all the suffering go away
Make myself completely numb
And get me through the day

How many doses can I have
To keep from feeling at all
Hours barley conscious
Not attempting to stand tall

What color is the pill
That will make me forget
The mistakes I made
Mistakes I still regret

Where is the bottle
Full of chemical magic
For me to consume
That will bring me back from sadness

Do I have enough
To buy a perfect remedy
So I can sleep past nightmares
And wake up with her next to me

Is there such a drug
To make me into what she wants
Her knight in shiny armor
A guy she loves to flaunt

Can I mix something together
So I can change
Into someone I should have been
So no one else will go away

(Sym)pathetic

I can still feel the fractures in my bones
But I'm still standing here all alone
Because you told me to wait
And we can restart our days

I fight through my state of atrophy
Just to make you a little happy
Hiding my pain with a smile
So you can relax for a while

You ignore my visible scars
And the loss of strength in my arms
I can barely hold up my gift to you
But you don't care what I do

As you leave your sickness behind
You also leave me out of your life
I still need some care
And you vanish into thin air

Dying Significant

I wish you could hear me
And see all I try to do
But I must be too quiet
Too insignificant for you

I am not being greedy
I just want to keep you safe
From the plagues and the vermin
That you always invite to your place

I can't keep saving you
From the fires that you always create
Stop consuming these poisons
There is only so much my heart can take

All of your tears that only I remember
Are enough to drown the world
But you keep listening to these bastards
And it's killing me, leaving me cold

One day I will vanish
And I won't be able to save you anymore
I love you to death and you know it
But you are not worth dying for

The Vicious Cycle

There you are
Just singing and smiling
Saying we should be together
And I fall for you

Here we are
Getting along so perfectly
But you say that it's not so serious
And you disappear

I have to walk away

There you are
Reappearing out of nowhere
With the same song and smile as before
And I fall again

Here we are
Better than ever
But you decided to change your mind
And crush me some more

I think I'm losing it
I think I'm losing it

There you are
With tears and apologies
Begging for forgiveness
Until I finally give in

Here we are
Where I always wanted to be
But when I close my eyes
You rip my heart out

I won't repeat this
I won't repeat this
I won't repeat this

There you are
I expect you to hurt me
But I miss that smile
And the cycle repeats

Here we are
We know what comes next
I give you what is left
And you don't hesitate anymore

I deserved this
I deserved this
I deserved this
I deserved this

Here I am
Waiting for you to need me....

Soul Displacer

Somehow it still lives
The same body as before
But now just hollow

Abyss

As I scream into this endless abyss
This madness
Godless indifference

I lose myself to what I try to suppress
Pure anguish
Sickened malevolence

The anger leaves and I just fall apart
A wounded heart
With broken parts

Weak and hollow I just can't restart
Use my arms
Or cover my scars

Home

Going home
To my dust covered house
The echoes are still there
Our broken promises still linger

Going home
To the ever empty castle
Where I am king
And you are so far away

Going home
To the remote island
Our eternal paradise
My new personal hell

Going home
To the distant cemetery
A tombstone meant for two
Now only my name remains

The Ashes Lie

The ashes lie
There was nothing here to burn
Nothing to light on fire
A pretend life made of air

The ashes lie
Her words were hollow
Nothing can grow from our remains
Or be resurrected with hope

The ashes lie
My scarred and calloused hands
Still search for the false love
Despite the constant bleeding

The ashes lie
Everything was insignificant
I mourn a pile of dust
Believing it was once alive

Detachment

The sheets with her scent
The clothes that fit her
I need to feel nothing

The ashes of the love letters
Empty picture frames
I want to feel nothing

Uncovered holes in the wall
The healing cuts from breaking glass
I struggle to feel nothing

Mirrors that had our reflection
A table just for us
I hope to feel nothing

A locked door we both could open
A view we both would enjoy
I will feel nothing

A breeze that would bring us together
The car that would take us on journeys
I start to feel nothing

Her number on my phone
The sobbing voice I used to believe
And I feel nothing

The apologies I deserved
Promises she should have kept
I am nothing

Sadness in her tone
Begging me for a response
Nothing

Numb

I'm supposed to be healed by now
But I'm still completely numb
Perhaps I've been hurt too many times
And this is the damage done
I'm now immune to the pain you give
And now I can't feel love

I should have just walked away
Instead of letting you kill my nerves
You loved how I made you feel
And now I don't even hurt
Try your best to apologize
You can't heal this love you burned

I don't think I am empty
I just can't feel you on my skin
Or warmth from you trying to fix this
I don't think I will feel you again
Good luck trying to find another true love
Knowing what you put to an end

Learning To Die Alone

I feel like I'm dying
Without you
And killing myself
To make you smile
You seem to survive
With or without me
While you are the first and last thing
On my mind

Those brilliant moments
When I'm happy
Are always followed by
The greatest pain
Those precious moments
When I'm needed
Right before
You throw me away

There has to be more
Than my pain for you
A better reason
To suffer
I should live for myself
My own path
Maybe if I look ahead
Instead of looking for you

The Zero Years

It hurts a little less
The constant suffering
Another day
Away from your shadow
Looking to the future
To my own life
I'm learning to move on
Learning to die alone

Older Ghosts

Closure can be tough
But your old ghosts will haunt you
Unless you stop them

Ghost Moments

Haunted for a breath
Just enough to ruin me
Some thought enters my head
And devastates everything

Whatever the trigger
I'm back in the past
Just the sorrow and punishment
Never the smiles and laughs

I am dead on the inside
Yet somehow I stand
Waiting for the ghosts to leave
So I can try to live again

Doesn't matter where
What happiness I find
They will eventually find me
And invade every part of my mind

Memories of long ago
When I was never strong enough
To face those living nightmares
When I was nothing close to loved

I fight those memories
And try to leave them behind
Their hands still digging into me
Staying a part of my life

No matter how I am haunted
I will not cause ghosts myself
No one I love will be haunted
I will not spread my personal hell

I will be a good memory
Until I become dust
Not a nightmare to invade a dream
Not a ghost that will corrupt

Blood Denial

I'd rather be an outsider
The forgotten bastard
To this hypocritical empire

I will not use your excuse
We were not born to cause harm
Don't expect me to take after you

Those footsteps you followed
Will not be the path I take
My life will not be hollow

I am exactly what you see
Nothing false to hide
I will always be me

My legacy will be my own
A life of honesty and compassion
No lies on my tombstone

False Eulogy

I don't know you
The one everyone respected
A perfect example to follow
Provider and teacher
I don't know you

I never saw you
The honest one
Hard working till the end
Proud but humble
I never saw you

I couldn't hear you
The insightful and wise one
Good advice for me to hear
Leader and giver
I couldn't hear you

I never found you
The ever reliable one
Selfless to the world
Honest and brave
I never found you

Death United

I miss you my brother
You were taken away too soon
I miss you my friend
And I'm too sad to move

I wish I could join you
Wherever that may be
I wish I could exit early
But that is not what you want for me

I will do my best with life
As hard as it will be to do
I will give my all to thrive
With the honor I learned from you

In death I will be united
With you and the legends of our past
And in death I will rest
Only after my time has passed

Train Wreck

I see the wreck
Before it happens
My warnings
Go ignored
Ridiculed
For trying to stop it
Trying to help

All the signs
So clear to see
In plain sight
My lungs
Empty and in pain
For screaming
At deaf ears

Pushed aside
My words diminished
And I just wait
For the explosion
So I can start
Picking up the pieces
Like all the other times

Never the hero
Never trusted
Despite all the wrecks
That I tried to stop
And the ones
I still see happening
Still preventable

As I leave
I try not to hear
The cries for help
I warned them
Before the wrecks
And I won't help
Any longer

The Day That Never Was

I lost somebody
That could have changed my future
Before we could meet

Lost Mourning

Somehow l lost something beautiful
I didn't know
No one said
Not even her

And I'm just mourning all alone
I'm so confused
Out of place
Just so damn hurt

What kills me is the future I lost
I would have tried
Gave my best
What could have been

The endless pain is now all I've got
I face the night
All alone
It does not end

A Day With Anna

The sun rises
And I hear you are awake
My little princess
You are ready to start the day

I open my door
And you greet me with a hug
I pick you up
To tell you that you are loved

Did you know
You have your mother's smile
My messy hair
But your own gentle eyes

Time to eat
Let's make your favorite food
Pancakes and eggs
So much that we will do

Let's go play
I will race you to the yard
Hide and seek
Tea time and sidewalk art

Time for lunch
Come help me make sandwiches
For our dessert
Some cookies with chocolate chips

Back outside
Hold my had as we take a walk
The perfect day
Let's go to your favorite park

On the swings
I push you as high as I can
Down the slide
Then I watch you play in the sand

Let's go home
As the sun starts to set
Eat some more
Then we get you ready for bed

Your favorite book
The end of a perfect day
My baby girl
You are my saving grace

As you sleep
I kiss your head and say goodnight
The day is done
And it's time to turn off the lights

The Endless Night

The night falls on me
And it only seems
To last forever
Morning never comes
I missed my one chance
To see the sunlight

But I will still live
And grow from this pain
I am not sure how
Or what will come next
As I move forward
In this endless night

You will live on
As a legacy
Somehow defining
In my own story
A belief of mine
That there still is hope

One step at a time
Is all I can do
Slowing my breathing
And gaining my strength
Before I get up
To face this lifetime

The Zero Years

The Disappearing Town

In the future ghost town
Where we had our laughs
Saw fireworks light up the sky
And the snow captured our footsteps

The memories of us begin to fade
Our heartfelt walks
Disappear into the road
Without us to walk together again

Many flowers that had witnessed our love
Have died many times over
Never to bloom again
Just like us

The walls that hosted our shadows
Have since faded in the sun
Worn out by too strong a storm
Like the promises we made

The playground we enjoyed
Has begun to crumble
Swings collect rust on their chains
Slides warp a little more every day

A house we used to walk by
The place we planned on making our home
Becomes just a cemetery
To the dead future we planned

The town will still exist
Without me adding memories
But I have no reason to go there
Since I no longer have you

For all I care
The town will fall off the map
A mirage on the road
Some place I will never visit again

Nothing Left To Grieve

The last threads of hope are gone
No reason to try and keep holding on
She got what she wanted all along

I don't know what all I lost
Rumors say that there was quite a lot
But I can see that I am not at fault

I'm tired of the sleepless nights
The lies and stress put on my life
And I'm tired of this pointless fight

Whatever I have to do
There's no winning for me to choose
So I better drop it all and start anew

A future alone is all I can see
Even though I have precious memories
I have absolutely nothing left to grieve

Discarded

This ugly jewelry was once beautiful
Shining promises
Before the neglect and tarnish
Took away all value

This pile of ashes used to be poems
Love put into words
Now just remnants of a fire
Worthless to the world

A broken toy had a purpose
Hand built memory
Corroded from the inside
And crushed to pieces

Those shredded shirts were once complete
My love you could wrap yourself in
Cut down to threads
No longer holding together

Some special box that once held candy
Sweet reminders of affection
Long ago consumed
The taste forgotten

A smudge on paper was a drawing
Dedicated hours of commitment
Crumpled up and thrown away
Discarded

Passing Through

I can't help but wonder
What they think of me
The innocent two
The ones that had no say

I wonder if they will remember
The games we played together
Our imaginary adventures
The cartoon voices I used

I wish they knew
How hard I tried to make it work
What I sacrificed so everyone was happy
And what I still wanted to give

They never saw what I had planned
What gifts I had waiting
Brand new and custom for them
And what they would have inherited from me

I don't know what I would say
If I see them years from now
Or if they would recognize who I am
If they were allowed to miss me

I'm probably some villain to them
Some evil creature according to her
Just a random temporary stranger
That was just passing through

Reconstruct

This is a chance to rebuild
To improve on what worked before
To reconstruct myself

With a newer outlook
On what made me
And what tried to break me

Limits have been met
And now they can be expanded
Beyond what they were previously

This is a chance to discard
To lose that dead weight
To filter out the poison

With a newer taste for life
And want for what improves me
And a greater distaste for sickness

Reconstruction has begun
With advancements in the plan
While still keeping myself intact

Counting Bricks

My hands on the wall
Trying to reach higher
And see if I can touch another brick

At least one more
Better than last time
Not wanting to lose any progress

My eyes staring up
At what I have built
And seeing how much further I still have

Just a few more bricks
Maybe a window or two
I'm still building
Still reaching up

Goodbye To Us

Goodbye to us
And what we had
Our beautiful love
Before it became sad
The bonds that we made
Became too frail
Just glass causing pain
Something that couldn't prevail

Hello to you
As you make your own day
With a smile brand new
And a feeling of being okay
The negatives are yours to fix
You can do it if you try
Instead of letting them get you sick
You no longer have to cry

Hello to me
And my new self-worth
The scars still easy to see
But without all the hurt
Using my new strength
To escape my collapse
And rebuild a better place
Where my heart can relax

As the clocks still move
We must do the same
With every path that we choose
We accept the joys and the pain
Our lives will no longer connect
With nothing left to trust
So good luck with your own sunset
And goodbye to us

The Zero Years

I measure my life
By when you were there
My life before we met
And after you put an end to us

Those years in between
Seem to not exist
The greatest joys
And the most painful sadness

I can now remember
That I lived before I loved you
I was different
Someone else

I started counting
The days without you
The change in me is apparent
From the time that never was

You are my zero years

www.ingramcontent.com/pod-product-compliance
Lightning Source LLC
Chambersburg PA
CBHW060926040426
42445CB00011B/806